City Firefighters

by Meish Goldish

Consultant: Robert Isbell, Fire Chief
Midland Fire Department
Midland, Texas

BEARPORT
PUBLISHING

New York, New York

Credits

Cover, © Photodisc/Thinkstock, © Stockbyte/Thinkstock, and © Mark Downey/Alamy; 1, © Photodisc/Thinkstock, © Stockbyte/Thinkstock, and © Mark Downey/Alamy; 4, © Bob Vonderau/Vonderauvisuals; 5, © Charles Rex Arbogast/Associated Press; 6, © Charles Rex Arbogast/Associated Press; 7, © John Gress/Corbis; 8, © Transtock/Corbis; 9, © STR/CHINATOPIX/Associated Press; 10, © Radius/Superstock; 11L, © Kristen Zambo/Racine, Wis. Journal Times; 11R, © City of Franklin Fire Department; 12, © mikeledray/Shutterstock; 13, © Florian Kollman; 14, © Tom Carter/Alamy; 15L, © dlewis33/Istockphoto; 15R, © Douglas R. Clifford/ZUMA Press/Newscom; 16L, © Condor 36/Shutterstock; 16R, © Terry Poche/Shutterstock; 17, © Tatiana Belova/Shutterstock; 18, © Marc A. Hermann/MTA New York City Transit; 19T, © Marc A. Hermann/MTA New York City Transit; 19B, © Monkey Business Images/Shutterstock; 20, © Mike Eliason/Santa Barbara News-Press/ZUMAPRESS.com; 20B, © Jeff Thrower/Shutterstock; 21, © Westport (Connecticut) Fire Department photo; 22, © Chris Collins/Corbis; 23, © Mario Tama/Getty Images; 24–25, © Hubert Boesl/Corbis; 25, © Blake Wallis/Barcroft Media/Getty Images; 26, © V Stock/Alamy; 27T, © Marmaduke St. John/Alamy; 27B, © Cusp/Superstock; 28L, © AP Photo/John Cetrino; 28TR, © IndexStock/Superstock; 28BR, © Paul Heinrich/Alamy; 29, © Design Pics/Superstock; 29BR, © Westport (Connecticut) Fire Department photo; 31, © Jerry Sharp/Shutterstock.

Publisher: Kenn Goin
Editor: Jessica Rudolph
Creative Director: Spencer Brinker
Design: Emma Randall
Photo Researcher: Ruby Tuesday Books

Library of Congress Cataloging-in-Publication Data

Goldish, Meish, author.
  City firefighters / by Meish Goldish.
      pages cm. — (Fire fight! The bravest)
  Audience: Ages 7–12.
  Includes bibliographical references and index.
  ISBN 978-1-62724-097-0 (library binding) — ISBN 1-62724-097-7 (library binding)
  1. Fire fighters—Juvenile literature. 2. Fire extinction—Juvenile literature. I. Title.
  HD8039.F5G64 2014
  363.37092—dc23
                           2013041503

For more information, write to Bearport Publishing Company, Inc., 45 West 21st Street, Suite 3B, New York, New York 10010. Printed in the United States of America.

10 9 8 7 6 5 4 3 2

Contents

Giant Flames!

Shortly after 9:00 P.M. on January 22, 2013, fire trucks raced through the streets of Chicago with their sirens blaring. A fire had broken out in a large five-story **warehouse** at the south end of the city. Nearly 200 firefighters were called to battle the huge blaze.

The fire was so big that it could be seen up to five miles (8 km) away. Heat from the giant blaze could be felt for blocks.

When fire **crews** got to the warehouse, they saw giant flames shooting out of the building's windows. The firefighters had to act quickly. The fire had reached all five floors of the warehouse and could easily spread to other buildings in the neighborhood. One of them housed a printing company with highly **flammable** chemicals stored inside. There was also a gas station nearby. If the flames got too close, the station's **fuel** could **explode**.

Firefighters began spraying the warehouse with water as soon as they arrived on the scene.

The Chicago warehouse fire spread quickly because much of the building was made of wood. A fire needs a fuel, such as wood or gasoline, to keep burning.

A Freezing Battle

Chicago firefighters had an extra hard time battling the huge warehouse blaze because of the freezing weather conditions. That night, the temperature had dipped to about 10°F (-12°C). Water that was sprayed onto the warehouse from fire hoses dripped onto nearby buildings, cars, and **hydrants**—and quickly froze. Fire crews struggled to walk on the slippery ground while carrying heavy, ice-covered ladders and hoses.

Ice covered the Chicago firefighters' gear and equipment, including their helmets, coats, gloves, and hoses.

Water freezes when the air temperature drops to 32°F (0°C) or lower.

Shortly after midnight, firefighters had the blaze under control. When the sun came up, the warehouse looked like a giant ice cube. However, fire crews had won their battle. They had stopped the fire from spreading to other buildings.

By the time firefighters put out the blaze, the warehouse was completely covered with ice. Luckily, no one had been inside the warehouse when it caught fire.

City Blazes

In big cities like Chicago, firefighters **respond** to many kinds of fire emergencies. For example, they may be called to a burning house or store. At some blazes, firefighters must not only **extinguish** the flames, they must also rescue **victims** trapped inside buildings.

City firefighters often use tall ladders to rescue people from the upper floors of burning buildings.

City firefighters often battle fires in **high-rise** apartment or office buildings. If the fire is on an upper floor, it may be too dangerous to take the elevator up, or the elevator may not be working. When that happens, firefighters have to walk up many flights of stairs while carrying hoses, axes, and other heavy equipment.

City firefighters battle deadly blazes all over the world. In 2010, firefighters in Shanghai, China, fought flames in a 28-story apartment building. More than 100 people were injured or killed in the fire.

In addition to buildings, city firefighters put out fires in cars, trucks, and buses. In big cities, they even fight fires underground in **subways**.

Fit to Fight

Because city firefighters have to lift heavy equipment, as well as carry victims, it's important that they're strong enough to perform their work. Job **candidates** must pass a tough **physical** test before they can start to train as firefighters. The test is divided into a number of tasks that need to be completed in a short amount of time, usually just a few minutes.

During the physical test, a firefighter faces conditions similar to the ones he or she might face in a real blaze. This candidate is strong enough to carry heavy hoses into a smoke-filled building.

Tasks can differ, depending on the city where the test is given. In Cleveland, Ohio, for example, candidates must carry 50-pound (23 kg) hoses up three flights of stairs. They also have to drag a 175-pound (79 kg) dummy a distance of 100 feet (30.5 m). In Franklin, Tennessee, candidates need to show that they can crawl through a narrow tunnel 30 feet (9 m) long.

Firefighter candidates also have to pass a written test and a medical exam. During the medical exam, doctors check for heart conditions, eye problems, and hearing problems.

A candidate crawling through a narrow tunnel

This firefighter candidate is dragging a dummy that weighs as much as an average person.

Fire School

If candidates pass their physical test, they can start job training at a fire **academy**. Nigel Defreitas and Peter Hespe were **trainees** at an academy in New York City. In class, the two trainees learned how fires behave differently, depending on the materials used to **construct** a building, such as wood, glass, or plastic.

Trainees also learn how to safely hold a fire hose so the force of the water running through it doesn't knock them over.

Each day after class, Nigel and Peter entered the "smokehouse" for a hands-on fire **exercise**. The smokehouse is a building where fires are set on purpose so trainees can learn to stay calm around deadly flames and smoke. Nigel said that in the smokehouse, "The heat is so **intense** you can't breathe."

A smokehouse in New York City

Station Duties

In the last weeks of training, firefighter trainees are assigned to a **fire station** to learn how to perform daily tasks. Fire stations are buildings where firefighters prepare for their next emergency. Nigel and Peter performed many duties there. They washed the fire trucks and filled their giant tanks with 500 gallons (1,893 l) of water.

Firefighters keep trucks clean and ready for the next fire call.

Since firefighters eat at the station, Nigel and Peter washed dishes, too. Another firefighter at the station, Frank Campisi, says that every job a trainee does is important. "This shows us the kind of person you are," he explains. "If we can depend on you here, then we can expect a lot of good things from you on the fire floor, too."

Firefighters spend part of their time at the station exercising to stay in shape.

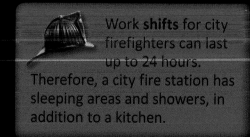

Work **shifts** for city firefighters can last up to 24 hours. Therefore, a city fire station has sleeping areas and showers, in addition to a kitchen.

Working as a Team

By living together at a fire station, city firefighters feel that they're part of a team. The group of station workers, called a company, is led by a **battalion** chief. During a fire, the chief assigns jobs to different company members, such as setting up ladders or attaching hoses to hydrants.

Firefighters work in teams to perform tasks such as spraying water from a hose or setting up a ladder to rescue people in a building.

When putting out a fire, company members may have to do more than one job. Therefore, each firefighter must know how to perform every kind of task.

Working as a team helps firefighters stay safe on the job. They never enter a burning building alone. Instead, each company member always stays with one or more fellow firefighters. Partners check on one another to make sure they are safe at all times.

These two firefighters are carrying a person from a burning building.

Deadly Smoke

While city firefighters try to stay safe on the job, they always face the danger of breathing in **toxic** smoke. In May 2013, a garage fire broke out in a crowded part of New York City called the Bronx. Flames spread quickly to nearby stores and apartment buildings. Huge clouds of smoke filled the air for blocks. Many **residents** pulled their shirts over their noses and ran away from the smoke.

After most of the smoke had cleared, firefighters were lifted above the buildings by a fire truck ladder to spray water on any remaining flames below.

The firefighters who helped put out the blaze wore face masks as they sprayed water on the flames, but this only blocked out some of the smoke. Eleven firefighters still had to be **treated** for smoke **inhalation**. To keep other people safe from the smoke, trains were ordered to stop running through the neighborhood. Students at nearby schools were told to go home.

Many buildings were destroyed in the Bronx fire. Thanks to the firefighters' efforts, however, no one was killed.

Smoke inhalation is the most common cause of death from a fire. When smoke fills the air with poisonous gases, a person can't get enough **oxygen**. In just a few seconds, a person can pass out and even die.

The Bronx firefighters used face masks like these to block out some of the toxic smoke as they worked.

More Than Fires

City firefighters do more than just put out fires. They also rescue people in other types of emergencies. After a traffic accident, firefighters may need to free someone trapped inside a crushed **vehicle**. If the car doors won't open, firefighters use a special tool called the Jaws of Life to cut off the doors or roof to get the victim out.

After a traffic accident in Southern California, this car was in danger of falling off a 100-foot (30.5 m) bridge. Firefighters were able to rescue a woman and her two daughters trapped inside.

The Jaws of Life works like

Firefighters even rescue animals in trouble. In February 2013, firefighter Tobias Ostapchuk helped a dog that had fallen into an icy pond in Westport, Connecticut. The dog, Huckleberry, clung to a chunk of ice with its paws but was too weak to climb out of the water. Tobias entered the freezing pond, swam to the shivering dog, and in no time, lifted Huckleberry to safety.

Firefighter Tobias Ostapchuk with Huckleberry

Tobias wore a special suit to protect him from the freezing

A Terrible Day

Despite brave efforts, city firefighters aren't always able to rescue everyone in an emergency. On the morning of September 11, 2001, **terrorists** flew two airplanes into the north and south towers of the World Trade Center, known as the Twin Towers, in New York City. Jet fuel in the planes exploded, starting **scorching** fires inside the two buildings.

Fire companies from across the city raced to the scene to try to rescue people who were trapped inside the flaming towers. Wearing full gear, the firefighters started marching up the stairs to reach the blazes. One firefighter, Marcel Claes, made it as high as the 35th floor in the north tower when a battalion chief ordered, "Drop everything and get out!"

Just before Marcel was ordered to get out of the north tower, he heard a loud rumbling that "felt like an earthquake." It was the sound of the south tower **collapsing**.

These rescue workers are helping a fellow firefighter who was injured when he tried to save others on September 11.

23

Race to Escape

Following the chief's orders, Marcel immediately turned around and headed back down the stairs. When he reached the street, he looked up and saw that the north tower was collapsing. Marcel ran for his life. As the building crashed down, his throat filled with ash from the burning towers, but thankfully he was alive.

When the Twin Towers collapsed, giant clouds of smoke and dust spread for blocks.

Marcel and other firefighters immediately began putting out small fires on the ground and digging through the **rubble** for possible survivors. Only 20 people trapped in the rubble were found alive. About 2,800 victims died in the World Trade Center attack, including 343 firefighters who were trapped inside the towers when they collapsed.

Many firefighters worked with search dogs to try to find survivors trapped under the rubble of the collapsed buildings.

Why Be a City Firefighter?

With all of the dangers, why would anyone want to be a city firefighter? Bernie Gonzalez wanted to be a firefighter ever since her class took a field trip to a fire station when she was six years old. Today, she works for the Midland Fire Department in Texas. "Every single day you come to work, there's something different going on," said the young firefighter. "I love everything about it so far."

There are more than one million firefighters in the United States. About 40,000 are women.

Jimmy Senk of New York City's Fire Department once risked his life to pull a four-year-old boy from a burning apartment. Afterward, the firefighter said, "It's the greatest job in the world. You get to save lives every day!" With brave people like Bernie and Jimmy, city residents can always count on firefighters in a time of need.

A group of schoolchildren from Laguna Niguel, California, got to try out fire hoses when they visited a local fire station.

Saving lives is the most important part of a firefighter's job.

City Firefighters' Gear

City firefighters use different types of trucks to respond to many kinds of emergencies.

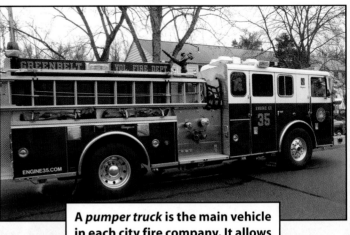

A *pumper truck* is the main vehicle in each city fire company. It allows firefighters to adjust the amount of water they pump onto a fire.

An *aerial truck* has a long ladder that is used to fight fires in tall buildings.

A *rescue truck* carries tools such as thick rope, poles, and the Jaws of Life, which may be needed to save people who are trapped.

City firefighters use and wear special equipment on the job. Here is some of their gear.

The *helmet* is made of strong plastic that will not easily melt in a fire. Fire-resistant flaps protect the wearer's neck and ears.

The *turnout coat* protects the firefighter from flames.

The *face mask* helps the firefighter breathe easily by blocking out smoke.

An *ax* is used to break through walls and doors.

Gloves are fire resistant.

The *air tank* holds enough air for the firefighter to breathe for about 15 to 30 minutes.

A *two-way radio* allows firefighters to stay in touch with one another while working.

Bunker pants protect a firefighter from getting burned on the legs.

Boots are so strong that it is difficult for nails or other sharp objects to puncture them.

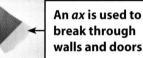

Glossary

academy (uh-KAD-uh-mee) a school that teaches special subjects or skills

battalion (buh-TAL-yuhn) a large group organized to work together

candidates (KAN-duh-dayts) people who are hoping to get a certain job

collapsing (kuh-LAPS-ing) falling down or caving in

construct (kuhn-STRUHKT) to build or make something

crews (KROOZ) teams of people who work together to get a job done

exercise (EK-sur-*syez*) an activity that is used for training

explode (ek-SPLOHD) to blow apart with a loud bang and great force

extinguish (ek-STING-wish) to put out a fire

fire station (FIRE STAY-shuhn) a building where fire equipment is kept and where firefighters wait for their next emergency call

flammable (FLAM-uh-buhl) able to easily catch fire

fuel (FYOO-uhl) something that is burned to produce heat or energy, such as wood, coal, or gasoline

high-rise (HYE-*rize*) having several stories and elevators

hydrants (HYE-druhnts) large outdoor pipes, connected to a water supply, that are used in a fire emergency

inhalation (in-huh-LAY-shuhn) the act of breathing in

intense (in-TENSS) very strong

oxygen (OK-suh-juhn) a colorless, odorless gas found in the air and water, which people and animals need to breathe

physical (FIZ-uh-kuhl) having to do with the body

residents (REZ-uh-duhnts) people who live in a particular place

respond (ri-SPOND) to arrive at the scene of an emergency to provide help

rubble (RUHB-uhl) pieces of broken concrete, bricks, and other building materials

scorching (SKORCH-ing) extremely hot

shifts (SHIFTS) set periods of time in which people work

subways (SUHB-*wayz*) electric trains that run underground in a city

terrorists (TER-ur-ists) individuals or groups that use violence and terror to get what they want

toxic (TOK-sik) poisonous

trainees (tray-NEEZ) people who are learning a new skill

treated (TREET-ihd) given medical care

vehicle (VEE-uh-kuhl) something that carries people or goods from one place to another, such as a car or truck

victims (VIK-tuhmz) people who have been hurt or killed

warehouse (WAIR-*hous*) a large building used for storing goods or merchandise

Bibliography

Fire Department of the City of New York:
www.nyc.gov/html/fdny/html/home2.shtml

Halberstam, David. *Firehouse*. New York: Hyperion (2002).

Pickett, George. *The Brave: A Story of New York City's Firefighters*. New York: Brick Tower (2002).

Unger, Zac. *Working Fire: The Making of an Accidental Fireman*. New York: Penguin (2004).

Read More

Goldish, Meish. *Firefighters to the Rescue (The Work of Heroes: First Responders in Action)*. New York: Bearport (2012).

Greene, Jacqueline Dembar. *The 2001 World Trade Center Attack (Code Red)*. New York: Bearport (2007).

Kalman, Bobbie. *Firefighters to the Rescue! (My Community and Its Helpers)*. New York: Crabtree (2005).

Thompson, Lisa. *Battling Blazes: Have You Got What It Takes to Be a Firefighter? (On the Job)*. Minneapolis, MN: Compass Point (2008).

Learn More Online

To learn more about city firefighters, visit
www.bearportpublishing.com/FireFight

Index

About the Author

Meish Goldish has written more than 200 books for children.
His book *Disabled Dogs* was a Junior Library Guild Selection in 2013.
He lives in Brooklyn, New York.